Finding My Voice

Angelique Presidente

Presentation by *BookLeaf Publishing*

Web: www.bookleafpub.com

E-mail: info@bookleafpub.com

ISBN: 9789358367157

First edition 2023

ACKNOWLEDGEMENT

Thank you to CORA for helping me advocate for myself! Without their help, I wouldn't have been able to find my voice.

COMMUNITY OVERCOMING
RELATIONSHIP ABUSE (CORA)
www.corasupport.org

Exhaustion

An overflowing river takes everything around it downstream, and now it cannot hold everything thrown at it.

When the river rushes down its path, it leaves behind what it normally would carry along.

Sometimes, the river flows so fast that it drags things along that wouldn't normally be affected.

During its tossing, twirling, and crashing, it wears away everything it comes into contact with.

As we reach our destination, the lake scatters all that we have clung to through the turbulent ride.

The overflowing river has reached its end and cannot contain all it held in its clenches. It can finally rest and find calm.

Meditation

When I close my eyes, I envision the life that awaits me.

At this moment, I feel liberated, free to be happy, and seen.

I do not hear thoughts that tear me down.

I am not constantly scrutinized and pushed around.

No, I live happily, in love, and with help.

The weight finally lifted, and nothing terrible to tell.

With my eyes closed, my world is finally up to me. I can focus on my children and how life should be.

As my eyes shut the slate is finally wiped clean, love, partnership, and relief can be seen.

I wish I could keep my eyes closed forever and I could continue to live in that dream. However,

As they open up to my reality, these moments are always abruptly taken from me.

I Am

I am from Sunday dinners with family but weekdays alone.

I am from a family member who says shhh don't tell or else.

I am from what seemed like endless days of toxic micromanagement to finally having the freedom that leaves me lonely.

I am from hardwork, endless days and guilt from working more than I see my child.

I am from being the only one I can rely on and always wishing I could have a break.

I am from being both masculine and feminine, praying one day I can submit to relief.

I am from intrusive thoughts that are not my own and fears that I was compelled to accept.

I am from the depths of a broken heart, as I yearn for the final goodbye I was denied. However, I also wish I never had to say goodbye at all.

I am from protecting my family from those who hurt us, as well as from exhaustion due to constantly looking over my shoulder in fear.

I am from a place that doesn't change no matter how much I wish or pray.

Life Gets Better

When the world seems dark, overwhelming, and draining, always remember that life gets better.

Life gets better when pain takes over and you feel alone.

When you have too much inside to let out and it slowly eats at your soul, life gets better.

Life gets better when you find your voice.

Life gets better when you finally break free from draining toxicity.

Life gets better when you stand up and decide to light your light again.

So, when you feel confused and lose hope for tomorrow, please, please remember life gets better.

Loneliness

I yearn for the warmth of a hug that penetrates the soul, the energy it injects instantly.

The presence of a soul that accepts me and embraces my flaws through love and affection, a gift I still search for.

Loneliness is the strongest feeling, the one that sticks around making me cold and empty.

Loneliness smacks me into my reality ripping me away from a fantasy life of love that I can never seem to grasp.

The broken promises, the actions that never match the words, loneliness seems to be the only consistent one.

The shadow of being alone is hungry and slowly gnaws at my heart. Soon nothing will be left but the shadow of a woman who has never experienced the magic of a partnership or true love.

The overwhelming anxiety consumes my thoughts as time ticks away.

Loneliness accelerates life and slows it down strangely at the same time.

When will I get the chance to experience reciprocated love filled with respect, trust, and affection?

When will I feel the warmth of love and affection instead of the loneliness of my choices?

When will somebody finally see me and my worth and not discount all I have to offer?

Silence Doesn't Live Here Anymore

The screaming, sharp words, and insults that pierce the depths of the heart - silence doesn't live here anymore.

The fear of another toxic encounter slowly hovers within - silence doesn't live here anymore.

The threats of taking my kids away, my everything in life, and leaving nothing but noise in my head - silence doesn't live here anymore.

Choking out my voice and my life in anger, creating flashbacks that never go away - silence doesn't live here anymore.

Silence no longer invades my voice or strength.

Silence no longer threatens my peace or safety.

Silence is now pushed aside; my voice is finally loud enough; it's heard and understood. - silence doesn't live here anymore!

Where Are You?

As I sit alone, I can't help but wonder if love will ever find me.

Will I find that exceptional person in my life who reciprocates my love and devotion?

I have waited decades for that special someone to reflect the same level of love I can offer. Where are you?

Where are you when my heart yearns for affection and someone to stand by my side?

Where are you when I have so much to talk about but nobody to tell?

Where are you when I only want a warm embrace and comfort knowing I am protected in somebody's arms? Instead, I am alone and cold without anybody to turn to.

Someday I hope you find me and bring with you all of the love and devotion I have yet to experience in this lifetime. However, I have given freely.

Until then, I will sit here alone wondering where are you.?

The Rose

The rose grew from a tiny bud and opened its pure petals to the sun's warmth. It hopes to be appreciated for its beauty.

As the rose flourished from the nutrients of its soil and water from the birds splashing next to it, it still longed for praise and admiration from its surroundings.

Slowly the rose started to fade and its ability to maintain its beauty lessened with the day. The rose could not understand why nobody admired it or smelled its pleasant fragrance and discouragement increased every day.

When the rose petals dropped and the leaves dried out, the rose told itself it was beautiful. It believed it was meant for someone to love.

The rose could not understand what was happening or how it could change itself to be loved by another.

Another rose bloomed next to it. It saw how tall and beautiful this rose was and admired what it would become someday.

With the first rose shriveling, the new rose
flourished, soon wondering about its own
beauty.

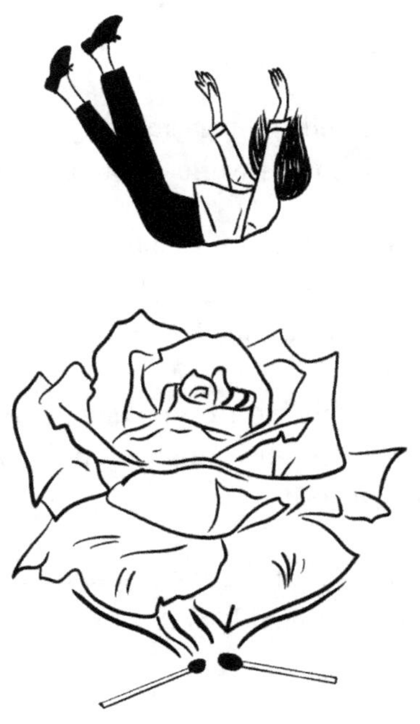

When Is It My Turn?

When is it my turn to feel love and happiness without pain and hatred?

A love so pure and innocent that it lasts a lifetime and hugs my soul for eternity.

When is it my turn to be heard and seen as the woman I am and not just seen without being heard?

My laughter and enthusiasm as I offer to share my vulnerable parts while embracing his.

When is it my turn to live and enjoy life without limitations or worries about how it will hurt someone else to see me happy?

As I let go of my worries holding me back from being free, I shed the chains inhibiting me from being my true self.

When is it my turn to have a happily-ever-after and enjoy true mutual love?

So far, this lifetime has only shown me the
negative side of my path and left me broken
without hope for the future.

When is it my turn?

When Will I Be Heard?

When will my truth be seen and not disregarded
the same way my voice has been all these years?

When will the pain I felt and feel matter enough
to be seen but also understood?

When will his lies be exposed and his faults
finally be seen without prejudice to his past
anguish?

When will the heartache of my silence resolve
and the voice speaking the truth be loud enough
to be heard?

Will it take me screaming on rooftops during the
night's calm?

When will I be heard?

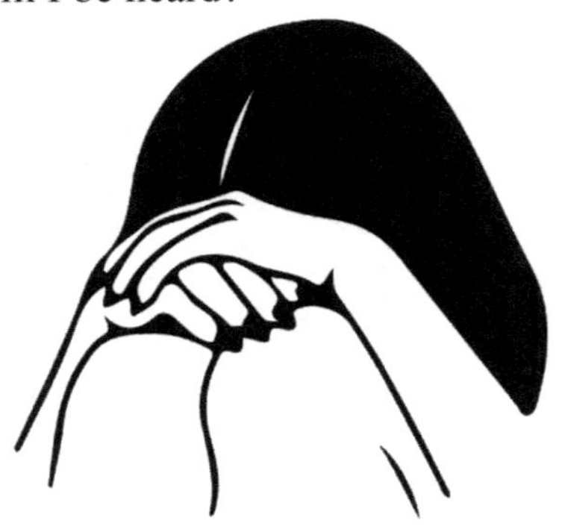

The Journey

As I have taken this long walk through the darkness that sometimes allows light, I seem to have always carried weight with me. I never knew how to disown it.

Through the twists and turns that this road kept bringing me through I sometimes learned how to navigate myself better later. However, not without giving up something of myself in return.

As this journey continues, I slowly find the packages I left behind. These packages are finally discovered as a result of acceptance by my soul.

Although the journey ahead seems daunting, I now accept that the light is brighter and stays longer. I open up to exploring routes that lead me to a path no longer riddled with hurdles from the past.

The present and future are brighter now but not without some darkness still lingering and trying to persuade me to change paths.

Dear 7 Years

Despite sometimes smiling, I was weakened by abuse and constant fear of being belittled.

I missed out on a life that I will never get back. Even though I could breathe, I never truly felt free or valuable.

When I think of what could have been or what I was held back from, it only adds to the heartache and confusion of how I ended up at this point.

So many choices I could have made if I didn't feel so powerless, lost, and micromanaged.

Will I find the love and happiness I long for from somebody other than myself?

That gentle touch, the warmth and understanding at this point I have never had in my life.

When will I finally be heard and understood in a way only my true love could offer?

Perhaps my time passed as I stayed imprisoned in a reality that blocked me from my true potential. However, I had all of life's golden possibilities all along.

Now I just long for a life that never seems to come true.

As a result of living a life that always has an emptiness.

Opened

I am opening now.

My future has been focused by the light I see.

I am opening now as the clouds of my past clear to let the light shine through.

I am opening now. I can hear a voice whispering and directing me in the right direction, but it isn't always heard over the shouting.

I am opening now and those around me can see me shine and the tarnish of the past is finally cleared off.

When I have opened completely the world around me will be the peace I have yearned for. I will no longer crave that thin ray of light that barely appears in all of this darkness.

When I have opened nobody will be able to take away the light again.

Anxiety

She watches me, judging my every move, and never lets me breathe alone.

She overpowers my voice and movements to make them her own.

I hope she finds someone else to bother with or maybe just leaves me alone. I want to be free from her tight grip and in complete control.

Her presence has never helped me. She silences me when I need to speak and makes me second-guess my words and emotions when I finally open up.

Hopefully, I'll remember how to find myself when I'm free.

The Game

I never win this game! My hope stays strong but then gets overwhelmed with despair and the background noise from the game's contestants seems to shout for me to fail.

The game noise is too loud to ignore. It takes my hope and crushes it instantly.

Those in the game get wild and laugh and cheer as my dreams get crushed quickly along with my meaning and reputation.

The game just keeps rolling me over and spitting me out like a tsunami blasting through a small city. It washes everything away in sight.

Once again, I must start the game over, beginning this quest at level 1. However, I must carry the burden on my back of all the previous levels I failed.

It gets more and more difficult to conquer level 1 each time I start over because the baggage of burdens grows heavier and heavier.

When will the game give me happiness or
peace?

When is it my turn to level up and shine among
all the other contestants in this game?

29

Love

I give love freely, but it's rarely returned

My heart feels empty and my future is blurred.

Why is it so challenging for others to show me
what I deserve?

When will I learn to stop depleting my own
reserves?

Lonely is my heart, my soul dim, my energy
faint

This time I wasted through life alone and broken
full of pain

Yearning for the day love finds me

Until then I cry, forcing myself to see this is
what my fate will be

An Empty Soul

It is only what I give that is seen by those around me. Nobody feels what I give.

With every act of kindness received, reciprocation seems further away.

My cup never being replenished, my soul dying of thirst.

The drought I endure consumes my peace until I live day-to-day struggling to get by.

Yet I continue to give and receive nothing like a dog who greets even the most dreadful of masters.

Taking crumbs to escape the emptiness inside, passing time never to be repaid, the emptiness grows stronger with every new day.

Soon I will have nothing left to give, and nobody to help me.

My Voice

My voice seems to be loud and proud when it comes to others' injustices but quiet and meek when it comes to myself.

My voice is nowhere to be found when I need it most, hiding behind loud voices that slice my soul. Returning only to silent screams within screams only I can hear.

My voice gets lost and contained by those who twist its words, confusing its meaning and stripping it of real value.

My voice yearns to be let out and heard but never gets the chance to be understood even when those around me are finally listening.

My voice comes out as screaming at times, scarring my evolution and halting any elevation that it helped to produce.

My voice gets devalued, muzzled, and tortured but it speaks its truth.

If only my voice could defeat you.